Family Fun

by John Serrano

This is my mom. We like
to read books.

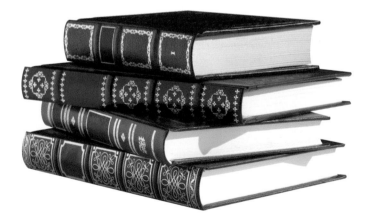

This is my dad. We like to bake.

This is my sister. We like to sing.

This is my brother. We like to make sandcastles.

This is my grandpa. We like to make airplanes.

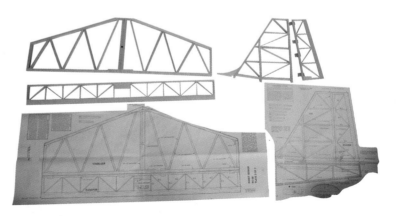

This is my grandma. We like to go boating.

This is my dog. We like to run.

This is my family.

We like to have fun!